THE
HISTORY
∞∞∞∞∞∞ OF ∞∞∞∞∞∞
LATIN AMERICA

SUSAN NICHOLS

Britannica
Educational Publishing

IN ASSOCIATION WITH

ROSEN
EDUCATIONAL SERVICES

Published in 2018 by Britannica Educational Publishing (a trademark of Encyclopædia Britannica, Inc.) in association with The Rosen Publishing Group, Inc.
29 East 21st Street, New York, NY 10010

Distributed exclusively by Rosen Publishing.
To see additional Britannica Educational Publishing titles, go to rosenpublishing.com.

First Edition

Britannica Educational Publishing
J.E. Luebering: Executive Director, Core Editorial
Andrea R. Field: Managing Editor, Compton's by Britannica

Rosen Publishing
Carolyn DeCarlo: Editor
Nelson Sá: Art Director
Michael Moy: Series Designer
Raúl Rodriguez: Book Layout
Cindy Reiman: Photography Manager
Nicole Baker: Photo Researcher

Library of Congress Cataloging-in-Publication Data

Names: Nichols, Susan, 1975- author.
Title: The history of Latin America / Susan Nichols.
Description: New York : Britannica Educational Publishing in association with
   Rosen Educational Services, 2018. | Series: Exploring Latin America |
   Audience: Grades 5 to 8. | Includes bibliographical references and index.
Identifiers: LCCN 2016058547| ISBN 9781680486834 (library bound : alkaline
   paper) | ISBN 9781680486810 (paperback : alkaline paper) | ISBN
   9781680486827 (6-pack : alkaline paper)
Subjects: LCSH: Latin America—History—Juvenile literature.
Classification: LCC F1410 .N53 2018 | DDC 980—dc23
LC record available at https://lccn.loc.gov/2016058547

Manufactured in the United States of America

Photo credits: Cover, p. 7 DEA/M. Seemuller/De Agostini Picture Library/Getty Images;
pp. 4, 5, 9, 37 Encyclopaedia Britannica, Inc.; pp. 4–5, 8, 16, 23, 29, 36 (background)
By Pyty/Shutterstock.com; pp. 10–11 Windmill Books/Universal Images Group/Getty Images;
pp. 12–13 Digital Vision/Getty Images; pp. 14–15 robert lerich/Fotolia; p. 17 © Victor
Englebert; p. 19 Jan Pešula; pp. 20–21 © Eli Coory/Fotolia; p. 24 ullstein bild/Getty Images;
p. 25 © Photos.com/Thinkstock; p. 27 DEA/G. Dagli Orti/De Agostini/Getty Images;
p. 30 Historic Map Works LLC/Getty Images; p. 31 Leemage/Universal Images Group
/Getty Images; p. 33 Jeremy Woodhouse/Digital Vision/Getty Images; pp. 35, 42 Bettmann
/Getty Images; pp. 38–39 Stefano Bianchetti/Corbis Historical/Getty Images; p. 41 U.S. Navy;
back cover by Filipe Frazao/Shutterstock.com.

CONTENTS

INTRODUCTION

Native peoples had lived in the Americas for thousands of years by the time the first European explorers set foot on their land. Although the Italian-born explorer Christopher Columbus was not the first European to reach the Americas (Vikings such as Leif Eriksson had visited North America five centuries earlier), the arrival of his ships in the West Indies in 1492 is an important milestone, since it marked the beginning of the colonial era in Latin America. Columbus, whose voyages were sponsored by the Spanish monarchs Ferdinand II and Isabella I, reached the South American mainland by 1498. Within decades, the Spaniards would locate and occupy the areas of greatest indigenous population and resources in Latin America. Other European powers soon followed.

But if these lands represented a "new world" for Europeans, they were a very old world for the native peoples Columbus and his successors encountered. These peoples included the Maya of the Yucatán Peninsula, the Aztec of Mexico, the Inca of Peru, and

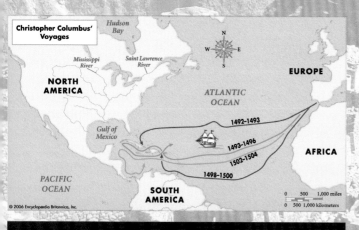

Christopher Columbus' Voyages

Hudson Bay

Mississippi River

Saint Lawrence River

NORTH AMERICA

EUROPE

ATLANTIC OCEAN

Gulf of Mexico

1492–1493

1493–1496

1502–1504

AFRICA

1498–1500

PACIFIC OCEAN

SOUTH AMERICA

© 2006 Encyclopædia Britannica, Inc.

0   500   1,000 miles
0 500 1,000 kilometers

This map illustrates the four journeys undertaken by Christopher Columbus and his crew across the Atlantic Ocean between 1492 and 1504.

Traditional Culture Areas
of the Americas

- Arctic
- California
- Central America and the Northern Andes
- Central Andes
- Great Basin
- Marginal Regions
- Middle America
- Northeast
- Northwest Coast
- Plains
- Plateau
- Rainforest
- Southeast
- Southwest
- Subarctic

A COMPTON'S MAP

This illustration shows the traditional cultural areas that existed in the Americas before the arrival of the Europeans.

many others. Their ancestors had arrived in Latin America some twelve thousand years earlier. Over the centuries, complex cultures had developed in the region. Large cities, long-distance trade networks, and sophisticated political unions arose, as did wonders of art, architecture, and astronomical knowledge. The temple-topped pyramids of the Maya and the stepped terraces and magnificent stone dwellings of the Inca, for example, attest to the tremendous achievement of these highly skilled peoples.

Tragically, under the effects of the European explorers and colonists, these native cultures suffered nearly total annihilation. Europeans enslaved large numbers of native peoples and accidentally introduced diseases to the Americas that decimated the indigenous population. Eventually, Spain ruled Mexico, Central America, much of South America, and parts of the West Indies. Portugal ruled Brazil. France claimed what is now French Guiana and several islands in the Caribbean. Many Europeans settled in these areas. They brought their languages, their Roman Catholic religion, and their culture to the region. Europeans also brought in many Africans as slaves.

It was not until the 1800s that most of Latin America gained independence from Europe. Spain's holdings in the region were largely lost between about 1810 and 1825 through a series of revolutionary movements. An outstanding Latin leader emerged during this period, the rebel general Simón Bolívar, who became known as El Libertador ("The Liberator") for freeing numerous areas from Spanish rule. Only the islands of Puerto Rico and Cuba remained as Spanish colonies, and these were lost in the Spanish-American War in 1898. Many of the new countries in Latin America set up governments based on the democratic pattern of the United States and France. Since that time, however, military leaders have often seized power, creating dictatorships in the region.

In the early twenty-first century, political instability still plagues some Latin American countries, and economic and social challenges remain.

This painting depicts Simón Bolívar leading his army at the Battle of Junin, on August 5, 1824, during the Peruvian War of Independence.

But increasingly, Latin America has assumed a more prominent role on the world stage. All eyes were on Brazil when it hosted the 2014 World Cup soccer championship and the 2016 Summer Olympic Games. In 2013 a humble priest from Argentina became Pope Francis I, the first Latin American to head the Roman Catholic Church. And in 2016 the president of Colombia, Juan Manuel Santos, received the Nobel Peace Prize for his efforts to end the decades-long civil war in that country.

Latin America continues to evolve and to fascinate. Its rich and dramatic history is presented in this volume, which provides a compelling look at the factors and events that have shaped this vibrant, ever-changing region.

CHAPTER ONE

THE INDIGENOUS PEOPLES OF LATIN AMERICA

Thousands of years ago, during the last Ice Age, a land bridge known as Beringia connected northeastern Asia to what is now Alaska. At least thirteen thousand years ago and perhaps much earlier, people from Asia began to cross over. These groups of people were the first humans to set foot in the Americas. (Later, when the ice sheets melted, the land bridge disappeared under the rising seas and the migration ended.)

Over several centuries, people spread throughout North America and eventually traveled down through Central America into South America. There, they established various cultures and identities. We refer to them as "Amerindians"—the first indigenous people to live in the Americas. They probably reached the southern tip of South America between three thousand and five thousand years ago.

HUNTER-GATHERERS AND NOMADS

At first, the Amerindians, or indigenous people, spent much of their lives searching for food, traveling around as they

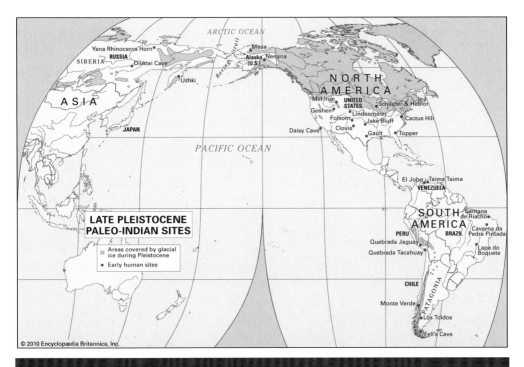

Early humans crossed from northeastern Asia to the Americas over a now-submerged land bridge over the Bering Strait. Archaeological sites suggest the migration routes of Paleo-Indians after the glaciers melted.

hunted animals and gathered raw fruits. If the food in a region was depleted, they moved on to a different area. In North America, for example, they stayed for a long time, but as game became scarcer, they followed the remaining animals down through the plains of Central America and the Andes Mountains of South America.

Life was dangerous for the early indigenous people. In addition to the hazards of surviving in a difficult time, they lived with large animals, such as mammoths, mastodons, and bison. Eventually, they began to settle on the land and cultivate it as they experimented with agriculture. All of this took place over the course of several centuries.

SETTLING DOWN

Eventually, distinct civilizations began to emerge. During the fifteenth and sixteenth centuries, the Aztecs ruled a large empire in what is present-day Mexico. The Aztec capital, Tenochtitlán, was a great commerce center. Founded in 1325 CE, the ornate city was built on a lake. It was also efficient; the Aztecs built aqueducts and canals that provided the

inhabitants with fresh water for food and crops, and a series of levees prevented flooding.

One of the most impressive indigenous cultures was that of the Incan people. Their empire was established in what is now Peru, and many cities were built on the highlands of the Andes mountain range. They connected their cities together by building paved roads, including suspension bridges to cross over the mountains. One of their most beautiful cities was Machu Picchu.

This artwork depicts a scene in which Aztec nobles and warriors survey the ceremonial center of Tenochtitlán. The structure they are gazing at is the temple of Quetzalcoatl.

THE CITY OF THE MOUNTAINS

The Incans had a sophisticated system of engineering and architecture, which is plain to see in one of their most stunning cities, Machu Picchu. Located in south-central Peru, 7,710 feet (2,350 meters) above

Machu Picchu, a famous site of ancient Incan ruins, is located about fifty miles (eighty kilometers) northwest of Cuzco, Peru, in the Andes Mountains.

sea level, and surrounded by the Urubamba River, Machu Picchu was inhabited in the 1400s and 1500s CE. It may have been a ceremonial site or the residence of the Incan emperor, Pachacuti Inca Yupanqui.

The city was surrounded by stepped terraces, which helped preserve the soil and distribute water. Many of its plazas, temples, and houses were built

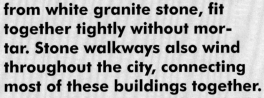

from white granite stone, fit together tightly without mortar. Stone walkways also wind throughout the city, connecting most of these buildings together.

One of its most stunning buildings is the Temple of the Sun, which has a semicircular structure. The temple must have been carefully planned by Incan architects and astrologers because, on the annual June solstice, a stone inside the temple is illuminated by the sunlight that pours in from a designated window.

Machu Picchu's ruins were largely hidden, having been overrun by plants, until a Peruvian farmer led an archaeology team to it in 1911. Machu Picchu was named a World Heritage Site by the United Nations in 1983, and it is visited by thousands of tourists every year.

DIFFERENT APPROACHES

The Lesser Antilles Islands of the Caribbean and parts of the South American coast were occupied by the Carib people. The Caribs originally lived in northern South America, but around 1000 CE, many of them migrated to the Caribbean islands. They brutally suppressed the tribe that was already living there, the Arawaks, by killing or enslaving many of them.

In Brazil, the Tupi people built a civilization that flourished. They first settled in the Amazon rainforest region, and they consisted of many tribes, even though they spoke a common language. One of the most revered indigenous civilizations was that of the Maya—spanning the Yucatan peninsula and Guatemala, it lasted over two thousand years. One of its most treasured ancient landmarks is the city of Tikal, where one can find pyramids that stand over two hundred feet (sixty meters) high.

These indigenous cultures flourished for centuries, rising and fading at different times, but the arrival of the Europeans in the late 1400s caused most of them to finally collapse.

The Temple of the Jaguar sits atop Templo I, one of the most impressive pyramids in the ancient Mayan city of Tikal, located in modern Guatemala. The temple rises 120 feet (37 meters), with nine tiers.

CHAPTER TWO

CONQUERING THE "NEW WORLD"

While we know that Christopher Columbus was not the first to "discover" the Americas, he did introduce the influence of Spain to the "New World." The early Spanish explorers who followed Columbus were referred to as conquistadors—"the conquerors." They were on a mission to find gold and become rich so they could return to Spain as noblemen.

The fact that there were already people living in these lands they conquered did not matter to the conquistadors. In fact, they used the indigenous people as slaves to mine for gold and precious metals. They defeated the people who were living on the Caribbean islands before moving inland to the continent. Within two decades after Columbus, large tracts of lands and many empires of the natives were being colonized—or taken over—by Spain.

THE REIGN OF SPAIN

The region of current-day Mexico, which had been home to the Mayans and later to the Aztecs, was conquered by

Hernán Cortés and his army in 1521. Peru's Incan empire was conquered in 1531 by Francisco Pizarro.

In eastern Colombia, ranchers take their horses for water on the Llanos, a large grassland plain. Horses are a common sight in the Americas today.

How did a small number of men conquer such a vast number of people? Although the conquistadors were outnumbered, they had superior weapons, such as swords made of steel, while the indigenous people's weapons were made of wood and natural materials. The conquistadors also had the harquebus, a type of gun that terrified the natives; the crossbow, which could send an arrow flying far; and—their ultimate advantage—the horse. Horses were unknown in Central and South America, and a cavalry soldier—a soldier on horseback—could easily dominate in battle against indigenous warriors on foot.

The conquistadors also unknowingly brought with them something much more deadly than weapons: germs. The viruses carried by the conquistadors devastated indigenous communities. The Indians of the Caribbean virtually disappeared. The estimated fifty million Indians living in the mainland areas at the time of their colonization had dwindled by the seventeenth century to only four million.

The people who survived soon found themselves enslaved, seeking out gold and precious metals for the conquistadors so that their lives might be spared. The conquistadors quickly set up an *encomienda* system, in which

WHAT ROLE DID SPANISH MISSIONARIES PLAY?

Spain began to influence the indigenous people in the Americas in other ways, specifically in terms of their faith. The Spanish colonial power believed it was their mission to convert the indigenous people, whom it considered to be godless, to Christianity. The Spanish were Roman Catholics, and they sent missionaries to the Americas to build churches and slowly convert the "new people."

The clergymen who traveled to the Americas represented many Roman Catholic orders, including Franciscans, Jesuits, Augustinians, and Dominicans. Their primary goal was to spread the Christian doctrine in the New World, as well as to promote Spanish culture among the newly converted.

Some historians believe that the missionaries made the conquistadors feel justified in their brutal treatment of the indigenous people. In fact, some missionaries converted natives by force. However, there is evidence that the missionaries often defended the rights of the natives and protested the policies of the conquistadors. Bartolomé de Las Casas, for example, traveled as a missionary to Hispaniola, an island in the Caribbean, and was shocked by the enslavement of the native people. He became a vocal advocate for the rights of the native people.

In Esquipulas, Guatemala, people assemble in front of a colonial Spanish-style church. The church is a popular destination for Christian pilgrims.

people had to present the local colonial official with the required amount of gold, silver, pearls, or other treasure, or suffer punishment or even death.

OTHER COUNTRIES, OTHER TERRITORIES

The conquest of Brazil by Portugal unfolded at the same time as the Spanish colonization of other lands. Pedro Álvares Cabral first landed in Brazil in 1500 CE, but he continued sailing west and reached Calcutta, India. The Portuguese explorers who followed Cabral were called *bandeirantes*—"flag bearers," whose mission was also to conquer. Like the conquistadors, they hunted for gold and other riches, and enslaved indigenous people to do so. About 50 to 90 percent of the indigenous population in Brazil died of disease, colonial brutality, or war.

The region around the mighty Amazon River, one of Brazil's most famous landmarks, was explored by Francisco de Orellana and Lope de Aguirre and eventually conquered as well.

The Monument to the Bandeiras is a large sculpture at the entrance of Ibirapuera Park in São Paulo, Brazil. It was sculpted by Victor Brecheret, who completed it in 1954.

Other European powers began to colonize the Caribbean islands after Spanish domination waned slightly. For example, the British seized Bermuda in 1612 and later colonized Jamaica in 1655. The French colonized several territories, such as Saint Kitts, Guadeloupe, Martinique, and Grenada, while the Dutch seized a group of islands including Aruba, Tobago, and Saint Croix, which came to be known as the Dutch West Indies in the 1600s.

CHAPTER THREE

LATIN AMERICA UNDER EUROPEAN CONTROL

Latin America during the colonial era, when European powers like Spain, Portugal, France, Britain, and others controlled its lands and people, endured a challenging and difficult time.

The Amerindians suffered from the colonizers' racism and watched as their societies transformed in unfamiliar ways. In colonial Latin America, the colonizers and their families formed the aristocracy, or upper class. They had money and wealth and vast tracts of land, which were often gifted to them by the monarch of their native countries. The indigenous people were subject to enslavement—and where they were not slaves, they were relegated to the lower classes. Their lives were dictated in every way by the colonizers.

POVERTY, SLAVERY, AND DISEASE

The life of a slave in colonial Latin America was not an easy one. Not only were slaves used to mine gold and other precious metals, but they were also exploited as agricultural workers, as much of Latin America became an agricultural resource for European colonizers. The Caribbean islands grew sugar, for example, while Brazil's land was used for coffee. These crops were then exported to Europe, keeping the European nations rich and Latin America poor.

The indigenous peoples experienced a dwindling in their populations because of their brutal treatment and the introduction of new illnesses, to which they had no immunity.

Women bend to collect coffee beans on a plantation in São Paulo. Brazil has been a main source for this agricultural resource in Latin America since European colonization.

This sketch, made in approximately 1880, depicts African slaves being forced belowdecks on a slave ship after being captured from their homelands along the western coast of Africa, known as the "Slave Coast."

But the European colonizers quickly settled on a solution: they imported a new group of people who would serve as their slaves, to "replace" the Amerindians. These, of course, were Africans. The trans-Atlantic slave trade is one the most terrible crimes in human history; over the course of several hundred years, millions of African people were forced into slave labor in Latin America.

The colonizers were quick to ensure that their new system of order—keeping African and native people oppressed and their own European comrades in power—would be permanent. They did this by creating laws that would prevent slaves and people in the lower class from

A CHANGING POPULATION

During the time of the European colonization of Latin America, the population began to change. For example, the Europeans and the indigenous natives sometimes intermarried and had children. The same is true of the Africans who originally were forced to come to Latin American as slaves. The colonizers attached certain values to each race. Before long, a system of labelling each of these new groups of people emerged.

The Europeans were referred to as either "Creoles" (*criollos*), that is, white people who were born in the Americas, or *peninsulares*, those who were originally born in Spain or Portugal and moved later to Latin America. Many Europeans refrained from intermarrying with indigenous natives or Africans; their full status as colonizers afforded them much more power and advantages.

Of course, any who did choose to mix with the indigenous peoples were soon given a new label. A class of people emerged who were known as *mestizo*, which means "mixed" in Spanish. This word was used to describe the children of both indigenous native and European parents. Mestizos could often rise further in social status than those who were indigenous, but rarely would they be permitted to enjoy the privileges of those who were fully European.

Another distinction was made to include people of African heritage; the term *mulatto* referred to a person who was of mixed heritage that included some combination of indigenous and European people with those of African ancestry.

Mulattos and mestizos form much of the current populations of many Latin American countries such as Haiti, Cuba, and Mexico. For example, in Colombia today, more than half of the population is mestizo and about one fifth is mulatto.

This eighteenth-century Mexican painting depicts a white man, a black woman, and a mulatto boy, illustrating the diversity of races in Latin America.

gaining any power of their own. For example, in some regions, a law stated that children born to a slave woman were automatically slaves themselves, owned by the same master who owned his or her mother. Other laws stated that slaves and indigenous people could not own land or property, keeping them dependent upon the Europeans.

TURNING TIDES

The colonies of Britain in North America defeated the British army and won their independence, forming the United States of America in 1783. Six years later, the French overthrew their monarch and his family in a brutal revolution, turning France into a democracy.

These two major world events—the American and French Revolutions—helped ignite a series of others, in which oppressed people around the globe began to seize their own freedom. The Latin Americas were no exception.

CHAPTER FOUR

REVOLUTION AND INDEPENDENCE

The movement for independence did not happen in one united movement, because Latin Americans were never one united group. Instead, it took place in a series of revolutions throughout the region, beginning with Haiti.

SLAVER'S BAY

When Columbus landed in the Caribbean in 1492, there were approximately one million indigenous people living on the island of Hispaniola (later divided between Haiti in the west and the Dominican Republic in the east). Within fifty years, because of oppression, disease, and the brutality of the Europeans, the indigenous population was nearly erased. (Even today, there is no significant native population in Haiti—it is mostly African and mulatto.) Spain took control of the island, populating it with African slaves.

France and Spain went to war over Haiti in 1793. A freed slave, Toussaint L'Ouverture, and other black commanders initially joined the Spaniards, but in 1794 he switched his allegiance to the French because France, unlike Spain, had recently abolished slavery. The Spanish were expelled, and L'Ouverture himself gradually gained control of Haiti. In 1801 his forces overwhelmed neighboring Spanish-controlled Santo Domingo, freeing its slaves and putting him in charge of the entire island of Hispaniola.

Though L'Ouverture was later captured and imprisoned by the French, the revolution he initiated to throw off centuries of slavery and oppression continued under his successor, Jean-Jacques Dessalines. In 1804, Haiti was finally liberated.

This map, dated from the 1800s, illustrates the city of Port-au-Prince, Haiti.

FROM SLAVE TO FREEDOM FIGHTER

In 1743, François Dominique Toussaint was born to a slave mother in French-ruled Haiti. He was legally freed in 1777 and formed a militia in 1791, with the intent of freeing other slaves. In 1793 he added the

A nineteenth-century engraving of François Dominique Toussaint, famously known as Toussaint L'Ouverture (1743–1803), leader of the Haitian revolution.

(continued on the next page)

31

(continued from the previous page)

word "L'Ouverture," a French term for "opening," to his name. It is said he was given this name for his ability to find openings in enemy lines.

Toussaint L'Ouverture fought for France during the war with Spain over the island, because France had agreed to abolish slavery. After France won, L'Ouverture became governor-general in 1796. Slavery was immediately banned in Haiti.

However, peace in Haiti was not longstanding; French leader Napoleon Bonaparte wished to restore influence and rule over Haiti, leading to an invasion in 1802. Now, the French demanded L'Ouverture's surrender—to which he agreed, as long as the French pledged not to implement slavery again.

L'Ouverture died in a prison in France in 1803, but the Haitians continued the fight, driving out the French forces in 1804. Although he did not live to see it, he had led Haiti to independence.

FREEDOM RINGS

Six Latin American countries in the northern region of South America can claim Simón Bolívar as their liberator: Venezuela, Colombia, Panama, Ecuador, Peru, and Bolivia. Born into a wealthy Creole family in Venezuela, Bolívar was educated in Europe in the late 1700s at a time when revolutionary ideas were sweeping the continent.

When Bolívar returned to South America, he helped lead many New World campaigns for independence, beginning in his home country in 1811. Despite many years of setbacks and failures, slowly these South American countries shook off the chains of oppression from Spain and became free.

In Mexico, the 1800s also brought independence. Mexican Independence Day is celebrated every year on September 16. On that day in 1810, a priest named Miguel Hidalgo y Costilla rang the church bells and called upon the poor and oppressed indigenous people to "recover from the hated Spaniards the land stolen from

A view of the waters of Lake Titicaca at Isla del Sol, in Bolivia. The island was an important center of pre-Columbian settlement.

your forefathers." Eleven years later, in 1821, Mexican army officers Agustín de Iturbide and Vicente Guerrero drafted a plan that would grant Mexico independence. Battles ensued against the Spanish army, but the Mexicans prevailed in August of 1821.

In Brazil, Portuguese rule was overthrown and independence achieved without much bloodshed. The king of Portugal assigned his son, Pedro I, to rule Brazil, but the prince declared the colony to be independent. He also named himself its first emperor, though he handed over the monarchy to his five-year-old son, Pedro II, in 1831; the child gained full power when he turned fourteen. Despite the relatively calm movement to independence, which was done without war or battle, life in Brazil remained a violent existence for the poor and the enslaved.

DESPOTISM REMAINS

Independence did not always equal true freedom or democracy for Latin Americans. In some countries, royal rule was replaced by brutal dictatorship. In Mexico, in 1876, Porfirio Díaz seized the leadership of the nation in a coup. He ruled Mexico for thirty-five years in an era that came to be known as the Porfiriato—a time period marked by corruption and the violation of individual civil rights.

In the Dominican Republic, power fell into the hands of General Rafael Leonidas Trujillo Molina in 1930. Until he was assassinated thirty-one years later, he enforced his laws brutally and the Dominicans suffered.

Just on the other side of the island in Haiti, years of revolution and instability plagued the country. In 1957

A 1959 photograph of President François Duvalier, who became the leader and, eventually, brutal dictator of Haiti.

François Duvalier became the leader, ushering in a horrific era of power made possible by the establishment of his secret police force, the Tontons Macoutes. After his death, his son, Jean-Claude Duvalier, continued his father's reign of terror until he was forcibly removed in 1986.

CHAPTER FIVE

WARS AMONG NEIGHBORS

T he late nineteenth and twentieth centuries in Latin America are marked by periods of prosperity interspersed with regional warfare. For example, in 1846, Mexico entered into a war with its neighbor, the United States. The Mexican War resulted in Mexico losing half of its territory (now the states of Arizona, California, New Mexico, Texas, as well as sections of other states) to the United States.

ON HOME SOIL

The bloodiest war in Latin America was fought between Paraguay and the allied nations of Argentina, Brazil, and Uruguay. The War of the Triple Alliance, or the Paraguayan War, lasted from 1864 until 1870, and it was primarily fought over borders. Paraguay suffered losses both in terms of territory and casualties. More than half of the people living in Paraguay were killed; a population of approximately 525,000 had dropped to 221,000 in 1871.

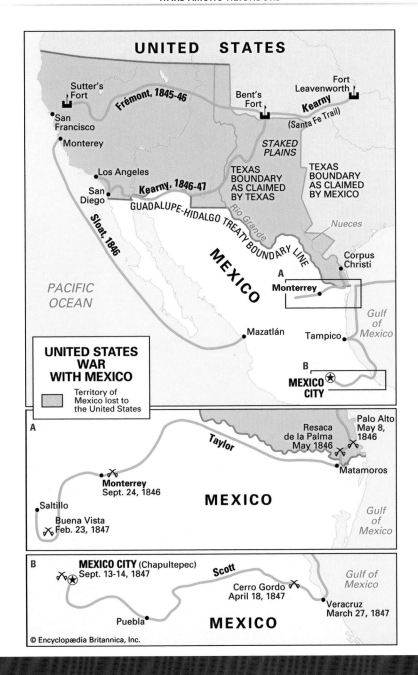

This map illustrates how much land Mexico lost to the United States during the war between the two neighboring nations.

SLAVERY FINALLY OUTLAWED IN LATIN AMERICA

Haiti was the first nation in Latin America to outlaw slavery, under the influence of Toussaint L'Ouverture, in 1801. By this time, three hundred years after Columbus's "discovery" of America, many European nations had already deemed slavery was a moral evil and were passing laws to abolish the slave trade.

Between 1824–1829, several other Latin American nations, which were slowly rejecting colonial rule by foreign powers, outlawed slavery: Guatemala, Argentina, Peru, Chile, Bolivia, Paraguay, and Mexico. Colombia, Venezuela, and Ecuador followed in the 1840s.

One of the last Latin American nations to abolish slavery was Brazil. Brazil was one of the largest importers of slave labor; about 40 percent of all slaves brought to the Americas ended up in Brazil, where they were treated brutally. Slaves regularly rose up to fight for their freedom, but their conditions were terrible and uprisings were suppressed. Finally, because of pressure from the international community and other Latin American nations, Brazil passed the

Golden Law, which abolished slavery in 1888. However, many historians argue that various forms of forced labor continued to exist in Brazil long after slavery was banned, which has led to vast economic inequalities among the population.

A nineteenth-century engraving pictures slaves washing diamonds as part of their forced labor in Brazil.

Between 1879 and 1884, Chile, Bolivia, and Peru entered into what became known as the War of the Pacific. The main issue was, again, border disputes, as most countries needed access to the Pacific coastline to export and import goods. Bolivia lost its territory that bordered the Pacific Ocean to Chile as a result of this war.

Sometimes, other nations fought wars with each other using Latin America as their theater of operations rather than their own soil. The United States and Spain fought such a war in 1898. The United States won the Spanish-American War, in which they claimed the territories of Puerto Rico and Guam. Cuba, which had sought freedom from the Spanish Empire, won its independence. Puerto Rico remains annexed by the United States, and Puerto Ricans are American citizens. The Philippines, a former Spanish colony, also fell under US rule as a result. The US built the Panama Canal to help move its naval forces across both the Atlantic and Pacific Oceans before giving up full rights to the canal in December 1999.

THREATS FROM WITHIN

Latin America has also experienced numerous military coups and civil wars in the last century. One of the bloodiest took place in Chile, in which President Salvador Allende was overthrown by Augusto Pinochet in 1973. The coup ushered in a terrible time for Chileans, as Pinochet was responsible for the murder, arrest, and torture of tens of thousands of Chilean citizens who opposed his rule. He was arrested in 1998 and would have stood trial for his human rights abuses, but he was declared

Small and large ships pass through the Panama Canal, a man-made waterway that is a vital connection between the Atlantic and the Pacific Oceans.

A 1983 demonstration against the government of General Augusto Pinochet of Chile. The demonstrators appeared at the funeral of fourteen-year-old Patricio Yanez, killed during a protest two days prior.

mentally unfit to defend himself and died before prosecutors could try him.

Cubans celebrated independence, but soon suffered under the corrupt governments of General Gerardo Machado y Morales and later Fulgencio Batista. In 1958, another revolt by Communist rebels gave control over the island to leader Fidel Castro. Castro implemented many socialist reforms, but people whose opinions differed with his policies were treated badly. Before long, many Cubans began to flee from the island to the neighboring United States. Castro officially stepped down as president in 2008, ending his nearly fifty-year rule of Cuba; his younger brother Raúl replaced him as Cuba's leader. On December 17, 2014, Raúl Castro and US President Barack Obama announced the restoration of diplomatic relations between their countries that had been suspended since 1961.

Drug wars have also caused difficulty for Latin Americans. Many illegal drugs arrive in the United States via Mexico, which has strained relationships between the neighbors. However, the emergence of drug "gangs" and the "warlords" who rule those gangs makes it difficult and dangerous to crack down on the trafficking of illegal substances. In Colombia, the illegal drug trade had often been a main source of income for rebel groups such as the FARC (Revolutionary Armed Forces of Colombia), which waged a long-running civil war with the Colombian government. In 2016 progress was made toward a resolution of that conflict when Colombian President Juan Manuel Santos and FARC leader Rodrigo Londoño signed a historic peace agreement in September; the country's Congress approved a revised version of that agreement in late November. For his efforts to end the civil war, Santos was awarded the 2016 Nobel Peace Prize.

GLOSSARY

abolish To officially end or stop something, such as a law.

agriculture The science or occupation of farming.

alliance A group of people, countries, etc., that are joined together in some activity or effort.

annexation To take control of (a territory or place).

bandeirantes A Portuguese term, literally meaning "flag bearers," that refers to Portuguese conquerors.

Beringia A land bridge that existed between Siberia and Alaska during the Ice Age.

cavalry A soldier on horseback.

civilization A particular, well-organized, and developed society in its most advanced stage.

colonize/colonization To take control of an area and send people to live there.

conquistador A Spanish military leader who traveled to the Western Hemisphere to conquer territory for the Spanish monarchy.

coup (political) A sudden and successful stroke or act to replace a country's leadership.

Creole Currently, this refers to a person of mixed European and black descent; in the past, this referred to Europeans who were born in Latin America as opposed to those born in Europe.

encomienda A system in which Amerindians had to present the local colonial official with the required amount of gold, silver, pearls, or other treasure, or suffer punishment or even death.

expedition A journey especially by a group of people for a specific purpose (such as to explore a distant place or to do research).

harquebus A type of gun or musket used by the conquistadors against the Amerindians.

indigenous Living, or existing naturally in a particular region or environment; the Native Americans were the indigenous people of the Americas.

liberator A person who frees or helps free a people or a nation from being controlled by someone else.

mestizo A person of mixed European and American Indian ancestry.

militia A group of people who are not part of the armed forces of a country but are trained like soldiers.

mulatto A person of mixed white and black ancestry.

native Born in a particular place.

peninsulare A person who was born in Spain or Portugal who traveled and lived in Latin America.

slavery The practice of owning slaves, in which people are forced to work and are unpaid.

trafficking Illegal or disreputable activity, usually commercial in nature (such as drug trafficking).

trans-Atlantic slave trade The segment of the slave trade that brought millions of enslaved Africans across the Atlantic Ocean to the Americas from the sixteenth to the nineteenth century.

FOR FURTHER READING

Baquedano, Elizabeth. *Aztec, Inca & Maya* (DK Eyewitness Books). New York, NY: DK Publishing, 2011.

Gibson, Karen Bush. *South America*. Edina, MN: Capstone Press, 2016.

Hirsch, Rebecca Eileen. *South America*. Jefferson, MO: Scholastic, 2011.

Koponen, Libby. *South America* (True Books). Jefferson City, MO: Scholastic, Children's Press, 2009.

Mann, Charles. *1493 for Young People: From Columbus's Voyage to Globalization*. New York, NY: Triangle Square Books, 2016.

Morrison, Marion. *Brazil: Countries Around the World*. New York, NY: Heinemann, 2011.

Pascal, Janet. *What Is the Panama Canal?* New York, NY: Grosset and Dunlap, 2014.

Petrillo, Valerie. *A Kid's Guide to Latino History*. Chicago, IL: Chicago Review Press, 2009.

WEBSITES

Because of the changing nature of Internet links, Rosen Publishing has developed an online list of websites related to the subject of this book. This site is updated regularly. Please use this link to access this list:

http://www.rosenlinks.com/ELA/history

INDEX

A

Allende, Salvador, 40
Argentina, 7, 36, 38
Aztec people, 4, 10, 17

B

bandeirantes, 20
Batista, Fulgencio, 42
Bolívar, Simón, 6, 32–33
Bolivia, 32, 38, 40
Bonaparte, Napoleon, 32
Brazil, 6, 7, 14, 20, 24, 34, 36, 38–39

C

Caribbean islands, 6, 14, 16, 17, 18, 22, 24, 29
Carib people, 14
Castro, Fidel, 42–43
Castro, Raúl, 43
Chile, 38, 40, 41, 42
Colombia, 7, 27, 32, 38, 43
Columbus, Christopher, 4, 16, 29, 38
conquistadors, 16, 17, 18, 29
Cortés, Hernán, 17
Creoles, 26, 32
Cuba, 6, 27, 42–43

D

Dessalines, Jean-Jacques, 30
Díaz, Porfirio, 34
dictatorships, 7, 34–35
Dominican Republic, 29, 34
drug wars, 43
Duvalier, François, 35
Duvalier, Jeane-Claude, 35

E

encomienda system, 17

F

FARC (Revolutionary Armed Forces of Colombia), 43

G

germs/disease, 17, 20, 24, 29
Golden Law, 39
Guam, 40
Guerrero, Vicente, 34

H

Haiti, 27, 29–30, 31–32, 34–35, 38
Hidalgo y Costilla, Miguel, 33
horses, 17

I

Incan people, 4, 6, 11, 12–13, 17
independence movements, 6, 29–30, 31–34
indigenous people, 8–9, 14, 16, 18, 23, 24, 26, 29
Iturbide, Agustín de, 34

M

Machado y Morales, Gerardo, 42
Machu Picchu, 11, 12–13
Mayan people, 4, 6, 14, 17
mestizos, 26, 27
Mexican War, 36
Mexico, 4, 6, 10, 17, 27, 33–34, 36, 38
missionaries, 18
mulattos, 26, 27, 29

O

Ouverture, Toussaint L', 29–30, 31–32, 38

P

Pacific, War of the, 40
Panama Canal, 40
Paraguay, 36, 38
peninsulares, 26
Peru, 4, 11, 12, 17, 32, 38, 40
Philippines, 40
Pinochet, Augusto, 40, 42
Pizarro, Francisco, 17

Portugal, 6, 20, 23, 26, 34
Puerto Rico, 6, 40

S

Santos, Juan Manuel, 7, 43
slavery, 6, 14, 16, 17, 18, 20, 23, 25–26, 29–30, 31–32, 34, 38–39
Spain, 4, 6, 16–17, 18, 20, 22, 23, 26, 29, 30, 32, 33, 34, 40
Spanish-American War, 6, 40

T

Tenochtitlán, 10
Tikal, 14
Tontons Macoutes, 35
trans-Atlantic slave trade, 25
Triple Alliance, War of the, 36
Trujillo, Rafael Leonidas, 34
Tupi people, 14

U

United States, 7, 28, 36, 40, 42, 43
Uruguay, 36

W

weapons, 17